blu

VIRGINIA GRISE

Foreword by David Hare

Yale UNIVERSITY PRESS   NEW HAVEN & LONDON

Yale University Press books may be purchased in quantity for educa-
tional, business, or promotional use. For information, please e-mail
sales.press@yale.edu (U.S. office) or sales@yaleup.co.uk (U.K. office).

Set in ITC Galliard type by Duke & Company, Devon, Pennsylvania.
Printed in the United States of America.

Library of Congress Cataloging-in-Publication Data
Grise, Virginia.
Blu / Virginia Grise.
p. cm.—(The Yale drama series)
ISBN 978-0-300-16922-5 (pbk. : alk. paper)
I. Title.
PS3607.R569B57 2011
812'.6—dc22
2011019727

A catalogue record for this book is available from the British Library.

This paper meets the requirements of ANSI/NISO Z39.48–1992
(Permanence of Paper).

10 9 8 7 6 5 4 3 2 1

All inquiries concerning stock and amateur rights should be addressed
directly to the author at vgrise@gmail.com. No stock or amateur
performances of the play may be given without obtaining in advance
the written permission of the author, and paying the requisite fee.

for the children who live under the blades of the
   helicopters,
trying to see stars through the smog, for that place
   where the horizon meets the earth
can you see it?

*imagine a world
   before war*

Contents

Create mini covers
for self study

find this

The Yale Drama Series
Lidless
Beu.

Need a
comments

Lidless

Foreword

The publication of *blu* in this beautiful edition brings to an end my tenure choosing the winner of the Yale Drama Series. I inherited the job from the founding judge, Edward Albee, and I am now content to hand it over to John Guare, confident that he will bring a special energy and expertise to the role. But before I do, it's worth recording how enlightening I have found the experience over two years of supervising the reading of 1,500 unpublished plays in the English language.

Sometime in the 1980s, I served briefly on the jury of another prize, exclusively devoted to plays by women dramatists. We scratched around for a long time trying to find a winner. The entries were worthy but dull. Now, a full generation later, it's remarkable how significant a majority of the best plays currently being submitted to this competition are by women. Frances Ya-Chu Cowhig won last year for *Lidless*, which as I write is about to open at the Trafalgar Studios in London, and now Virginia Grise has won for *blu*. Of the twelve finalists we short-listed in 2010, nine were female.

Clearly something is going on, and something which seems long overdue. Doris Lessing is clearly not alone in feeling that "I hate talking about literature in terms of men and women.

It isn't helpful." But on the other hand, many of us are dismayed to have worked so long in a theatre culture in which women were chiefly required backstage to wipe the brows of the male prodigies. Of course, the idea of progress in the arts is inherently absurd. Art is not a science which advances ever forward over new ground. Can Stravinsky's music properly be said to be an advance on Bach's? Is Ibsen an advance on Shakespeare? And, similarly, nobody of any understanding or experience would confuse art with self-expression. Even less is it therapy. The most propitious circumstances may not produce great work. However, surely we can at least say that the likely percentage chance of seeing interesting plays in a theatre will be hugely improved when half the human race don't feel themselves disadvantaged before they've even set pen to paper.

Like most people, I'm slightly embarrassed by morale-raising exercises in the arts designed to prove that a brave new world of progressive artists and audience is on the point of being created. With some rare exceptions—Joe Papp is the most obvious—the people who talk loudest about such ambitions are rarely the best at bringing them about. Of course, I want as many people as possible from as many backgrounds as possible to come to the theatre. But I also want the play to be good when they get there. Full theatres are great, but what if they're full of rubbish? In Britain, in the past twenty years, we have had a number of prominent arts organizations supremely skilled at ticking the aspirational boxes required by funding organizations, and rather less skilled at presenting plays. When I was growing up, after all, the greatest new dramas of the day were usually scorned by critics and prize-givers alike, and presented to near-empty houses made up only of a habituated middle-class audience. Yet in the fifty years since their elite premieres, those same plays have gone on to reach and inspire millions of people in countless languages all over the world. If, as I did, you shared with John Osborne's widow the experience of opening letters from teenage students in India who had just written in at the news of John's death to say that their lives had been changed by reading *Look Back in Anger*—a play first presented in a run-down four-hundred-seat theatre in southwest London—then you will know that plays, perhaps beyond all other art forms, often take a curious course, reaching out in ways considerably less programmed than any outreach programme could possibly design.

Be clear: all this is not the argument for the status quo, nor against the noble aim of attracting a younger and more diverse audience into the playhouse. But it is, on the contrary, a reassertion of an often-forgotten truth. In art, as in politics, the most profound change usually comes from below. A recent brilliant film by Clio Barnard, *The Arbor*, has drawn timely attention to the example of Andrea Dunbar, the playwright who, in the early 1980s, began to write in a school notebook the story of her life on a so-called sink estate in Bradford. She was a natural dramatist, with an exceptional gift both for structure and for dialogue, She has a notably unsentimental view of what it had been like to be born and to fight for survival in the most depressing of circumstances. *Rita, Sue, and Bob Too* remains her best-known work. But before Dunbar died of a brain haemorrhage at the age of twenty-nine, it was already clear that part of her eminence stemmed from her isolation. In spite of her exceptional talent, or perhaps because of it, she disturbed both theatre audiences and theatre-workers with an implicit question: "If I, a single mother from Yorkshire, can write this well about a way of life the theatre generally ignores, just think how many more uneducated young women there must be who, given half a chance, could out-write some of the theatre's most highly regarded playwrights."

It was a heady glimpse into possibility, and now perhaps at last we are beginning to see just a little bit more of that possibility opening up. I started out at a time when there were few women writing for the theatre. Even my legendary theatrical agent, Peggy Ramsay, about whom a number of admiring books have been written, disdained women and usually refused to take them as clients. "Women can't write plays," she would say. "Women write novels." She was mystified even by Caryl Churchill, whom she represented with a mixture of puzzlement and awe. What lay behind Peggy's view was the all-too-familiar belief that women work best in the realm of the private, that they are more expert in the inner life than in the outer. Jane Austen's unwillingness to make mention of events beyond the hearth while the Napoleonic wars were raging was always evoked as damning evidence of women's preferred field of operation. The fact that Peggy also acted for the novelist Jean Rhys did little to allay her prejudices.

So for me, then, it has been a special pleasure in both the years of my office to give this exemplary prize, sponsored by the DC Horn Foundation, to women who, among many other things, write about the impact of public events on neglected lives. Yes, *blu* is technically expert. Choral writing is particularly difficult in the theatre—T. S. Eliot is just one writer who repeatedly made a miserable hash of it—whereas, in performance, Grise's choral effects are thrilling and unexpected. But, just as important, the play uses a heady mix of Latino and musical influences to cast oblique light on people you don't usually come across on the English-speaking stage.

In celebrating the young female playwrights on either side of the Atlantic who are now adding some welcome provocation to the world of the new play—for once, we can say thankfully, there are too many to mention—it's impossible not to remark that the structures they write for seem some way behind. As usual, organizations are running to catch up with ideas. The question is: why so few women artistic directors? Or, indeed, so few women competition judges?

Although my own plays have lately benefited from being re-interpreted, often in fascinating ways, by a new generation of female directors who include Thea Sharrock, Indu Rubasingham, Anna Mackmin, and Rachel Kavanagh, it has been noticeable that they have, in every case, been reporting to male artistic directors. But, again, when I first went to the theatre in the middle of the last century, the fiercely independent Joan Littlewood ran one of the most original and accomplished theatres in the world at the Theatre Royal Stratford East, and enjoyed an international reputation beyond the dreams of any contemporary British director for doing so.

Now, with the expanding number of excellent women dramatists, let us hope there will also follow a freedom from any obligation for the depiction of their own gender to be either exemplary or representative. During the 2010 British general election, I interviewed the remarkable Birmingham Member of Parliament Gisela Stewart, who went on to hold her marginal seat, defying a massive national swing against the Labour Party. In answer to my question about her feminism she remarked, "I always say we will have achieved equality when we finally have as many useless women in Parliament as useless men." For myself, I believe, in the same way, that we will have grown up in the theatre only when women characters are depicted equally as weak and strong, as stupid and clever, as humourless and funny, and when playwrights no longer feel compelled to compensate for women's traditional underrepresentation by making them improbably virtuous. We may finally be heading towards that welcome tipping point when a single female heroine will no longer be expected to speak for all female heroines.

Both Frances Ya-Chu Cowhig and Virginia Grise are already in the vanguard of such a freedom in their different work. At a party in Battery Park to celebrate her prize, Virginia remarked to me how odd it was that an ageing white male playwright from Britain should choose two women winners, both of them from what are, in the United States, ethnic minorities. I replied it was hardly odd, because I hadn't chosen them. Truthfully, they chose themselves.

David Hare

La Ciotat, France

March 2011

Acknowledgments

I hold in my heart a deep gratitude to those people that have supported my work, my dreams and me—for holding me up, for helping me fly . . .

Joni Jones and the women of the Austin Project read the first complete draft of *blu* around Jackie Cuevas and Jen Margulies' kitchen table in Austin, Texas; Laurie Carlos let me rest at the Paris Hotel while I waited for the train to arrive; Adelina Anthony and Teatro Q created an unapologetically queer space for writing in the middle of South Central Los Angeles; Phillip Avila, Jessica Cerda, H. Esperanza Garza, Herminia Maldonado, Marissa Ramirez, Barbara Renaud Gonzalez, Maria Salazar, Deborah Vasquez, and David Zamora Casas literally kept me fed with both their care packages and love during graduate school, and Ricardo A. Bracho, Mirasol Riojas, and Alexandro Hernandez helped me find home in Los Angeles. Sincere thank-yous to Ron and Emma Grise, who raised me to be a dreamer, and to Janet Dreisen Rappaport for her generosity of spirit and tireless work to support the dreams of the next generation.

I'd especially like thank Carl Hancock Rux, who spent many hours across the table from me at a small coffee shop in Little Armenia trying to teach me how to listen to the voices in my head that talked to me in prayers and images and poems that I didn't always understand. I am grateful for his mentorship and friendship, for hearing the story, and for pushing me to work beyond what I knew, beyond what was familiar, beyond what was safe.

I would not be a writer if it weren't for sharon bridgforth, my Art Pa, who birthed and raised me an Artist, named me before I had named myself—for her unwavering support throughout the years, for creating an artistic family and home I could call my own.

Some of the initial writing for *blu* was staged in an evening of performance about education in the state of Texas, directed by Irma Mayorga. After that performance, I packed the writing in a suitcase and took it with me to California, where it changed radically by living in the East Los Angeles neighborhood of Boyle Heights. To the emcees Sistah Hailstorm and TIWAEIS and her three boys who lived with me in a two story house on Winter Street thank you for teaching me about family and giving me hope when I had very little left.

blu was developed in Playwrights Lab at the California Institute of the Arts, through their MFA in Writing for Performance program. Erik Ehn invited me into an incredible community of writers that continue to offer me support and guidance as I try to make my life as an artist. Muchísimas Gracias to: Brian Bauman, Karen Cellini, Sigrid Gilmer, Peter Jensen, Alana Macias, Sibyl O'Malley, Jane Pickett, Amy Tofte, Joy Tomasko, and to my sister elder friend, Deborah Asiimwe, without whom I would not have survived graduate school.

In 2008, *blu* was produced by CalArts as my thesis project, under the direction of Jon Lawrence Rivera with the following cast: Heather Alpert, Marlene Beltran, Justine DePenning, Julian Evens, Jessica Hemingway, Bianca Marrero, Chris Rivas, Nathan, Tenney, Chris Webb, and Tiffany Wunsch, with lighting design by Christopher Stokes and set design by Lianne Arnold. It received additional support from the Playwright's Center Jerome Fellowship, the Enye Project, the Ellen Stone Belic Institute for the Study of Women and Gender in the Arts and the Media, Austin Script Works' Head 2 Head Program, and the following series of staged readings: Los Angeles Theatre Center, directed by Maureen Huskey; Victory Gardens Theatre in Chicago, IL, directed by Marcela Muñoz; Yale Repertory Theatre in New Haven, CT, directed by Daniel Jaquez; Alliance Theatre in Atlanta, GA, directed by Susan Reid; New York Theatre Workshop in New York City, directed by Carl Hancock Rux; and the Vortex Theatre in Austin Texas, directed by Florinda Bryant. The following people have read the script in its various stages and have given me invaluable dramaturgical advice: Luis Alfaro, Daniel Alexander Jones, Lianne Arnold, Adelina Anthony, Erik Ehn, Liz English, Carl Hancock Rux, Mona Heinze, Maureen Huskey, Jon Lawrence Rivera, and C. Denby Swanson.

blu was also a finalist for the Alliance Theatre's Kendeda Award, The Kennedy Center's Latino/a Playwriting Award and the Princess Grace Foundation's Playwriting Award. I would especially like to thank Celise Kalke and Susan V. Booth for their commitment to the development of new plays and new voices for the American stage. The reading organized by Alliance Theatre at the New York Theatre Workshop with professional actors—including Karmine Alers, Stephen Bel Davies, Raul Castillo, Daphne Rubin-Vega, Dion Mucciacito, Gio Perez, and Carmen Zilles—allowed me to hear the piece in completely new ways and helped shape this most recent draft of the play.

I owe an incredible amount to everyone who contributed in some way to the development of this piece, even those whom I may not have mentioned.

Finally, I would like to thank David Hare, Francine Horn, and Yale University Press. As a kid, I spent many nights dreaming underneath a blanket of stars in San Antonio, Texas. Sometimes I wondered if those dreams mattered to anyone else but me. The fact that you could pick up this Chicanita's story, inspired in part by the young people I taught on the Southside of San Antonio, and "get it" without translation, that it mattered to you, means that we share the same sky, the same stars, the same moon even if we live oceans apart. From the depths of my blu moon heart . . . Muchísmas Gracias.

blu

Cast of Characters

SOLEDAD	mother (various ages from 15 to 37 years old). prison. tired of the hard life.
HAILSTORM	soledad's partner (in her 30s). two-spirited. ruff around the edges.
EME	father (various ages from 19 to 41 years old). old skool. black ink tat on knuckles.
BLU	older brother (18 years old). chaos and confidence. the coolest color.
GEMINI	sister (14 years old). would be traveler. dreamer.
LUNATICO	lil' brother (13 years old). lost/floating. spinning.

DOCTOR	played by BLU
COP	played by EME
HOMIE	played by LUNATICO
ESE	played by EME
RECRUITMENT OFFICER	played by EME
SOLDIERS	played by EME, BLU, LUNATICO

GROUP OF BOYS   played by EME, LUNATICO,
                            SOLEDAD, HAILSTORM

Time: Present day, looking back on the not too distant past,
through a series of memories, dreams, rituals, and prayers.

Place: The barrio. The United States of America.

Author's Note:
Style: This text, though rooted in real experiences, was not
conceived or written in a naturalistic mode. The directing
style, therefore, should serve the music, movement, and
mysticism intrinsic to the script.

There are moments when characters speak the same lines
and have the same memory. At other times, characters inter-
rupt and take over each other's monologues because they live
a shared experience. These voices should not be in unison but
should overlap, unless otherwise noted.

Music: Music (Chicano blues, colombianas, and urban hip-
hop) is a driving force in this play. The text contains breaks
and silences, loops and hooks. All sound should be run by
a live DJ from his/her turntables onstage.

Set: The stage should be a bi-level space, representing the
roof and the inside of the family's house—while separate areas
should exist for characters who interact on the streets of the
neighborhood.

GEMINI *is sitting on the roof alone, stares out into the distance. The earth and sky meet. The sound of helicopters passing overhead. The blades cut through time.*

Light like moonlight shines on SOLEDAD. HAILSTORM *and* EME *appear in separate lights, at different times during* SOLEDAD*'s life. She speaks to both. They speak to her.*

EME & HAILSTORM   what's your name?

SOLEDAD   soledad.

EME   like the prison?

SOLEDAD   like my grandmother. (*beat*). what's your name?

EME   my name is eme.

HAILSTORM   hailstorm.

SOLEDAD   like the gang?

EME   like my father.

SOLEDAD   like the rain?

HAILSTORM   turned ice, falls hard.

SOLEDAD   gang name, clique's name.

HAILSTORM & EME   naw girl. just a name.

EME   where you from?

SOLEDAD   here.

EME & HAILSTORM   where you goin?

SOLEDAD   nowheres.

EME & HAILSTORM   you gotta be goin somewhere.

SOLEDAD   why?

EME   stand still, the world moves round you.

SOLEDAD   don't sound so bad. like the earth. the moon orbits round the earth.

HAILSTORM   but the earth moves, spins on its axis in space.

SOLEDAD   wutcha know 'bout astronomy?

HAILSTORM   i know you can't see the stars in concrete. you gotta look up, soledad. the sky is up above not down at your feet.

EME   wutcha lookin at anyway?

SOLEDAD   the cracks.

EME   the cracks?

SOLEDAD   wonderin what makes the concrete break.

EME   where you live?

SOLEDAD   here.

EME   on the street?

SOLEDAD   i mean. not far from here.

EME & HAILSTORM   your old man know you out so late?

SOLEDAD   when'd you become my father?

EME & HAILSTORM   just wonderin.

SOLEDAD   i'm a grown woman.

EME   how old are you?

SOLEDAD   fifteen.

HAILSTORM   can see you grown. how old are you?

SOLEDAD   thirty.

EME   close your eyes.

SOLEDAD   what?

HAILSTORM   close your eyes, corazón.

EME & HAILSTORM   tell me, how many stars you see?

(SOLEDAD *closes her eyes, begins counting the stars on the back of her eyelids.*)

SOLEDAD   too many to count.

(*The sound of helicopters in the distance.*)

EME   sneak out your window tomorrow. i'll meet you here.

SOLEDAD   where?

EME   on the street.

HAILSTORM   meet me here tomorrow.

SOLEDAD   why?

HAILSTORM   let me teach you 'bout the stars.

SOLEDAD   i'm a thirty year old woman. wutcha gonna
teach me?

(*Lights on* EME *and* SOLEDAD *in the past.*)

EME   i dreamed it was a boy.

SOLEDAD   can't feed our son on dreams, eme. not enuf
to keep him full. you'll have to get a job.

EME   so will you.

SOLEDAD   but i go to school.

EME   not no more.

SOLEDAD   not sure i wanna be a mother.

EME   what?

SOLEDAD   don't know what i want to be.

EME   he grows inside you all the same.

SOLEDAD   seventeen year old mother and a bastard son.

EME   he's no bastard. he's my son. he'll have a name. i'll
name him . . .

*helps my daughter
name her son*

(naming

(EME *stops, takes off his chain and gives it to* SOLEDAD.)

SOLEDAD   what's this?

EME   a milagro.

SOLEDAD   y eso?

EME   protection.

SOLEDAD   don't need nobody protectin me.

EME   take it. (*beat.*) you ain't alone soledad.

(*Bright, sterile lights of the hospital room. Lights up on the*
DOCTOR, SOLEDAD*'s feet in stirrups.*)

DOCTOR   legs up. silver metal. this will hurt just a little.
clear gel on stomach. cold.

SOLEDAD   don't gotta do no tests. i know what's wrong.

DOCTOR   13 weeks. uterine. non-ectopic. you still have
choices.

SOLEDAD   wutcha mean?

DOCTOR   salt water injected into the amniotic sac. cer-
vix open.

SOLEDAD   tissue turns to bone.

DOCTOR   the tenaculum holds it in place. two, three
rods the size of a dime.

SOLEDAD   touch the feet and the toes curl down.

DOCTOR   very small. plastic tube with pointed tip.

SOLEDAD   touch the palms and the fingers close.

DOCTOR   cannula. pulled apart. sucked in tube. placed in bottle.

SOLEDAD   too shallow for him to swim. i carry the ocean in my belly. he swims inside.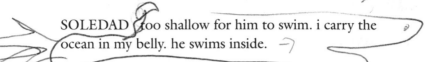

DOCTOR   what would you like to do?

SOLEDAD   i choose my son. (*beat.*) seventeen. when my first baby formed inside me. kicked and screamed and pushed up against my insides. flipped and turned and dreamed. inside me. underneath eyelids closed. i could see stars. day or night.

(*Light like moonlight shines on* SOLEDAD. *She begins singing, dancing alone.*)

(*singing*)

nunca me dejes sola y sin ti
que sin tu amor no puedo vivir
because i love you i love you i do . . .

(*Lights up on* BLU *in the past.*)

BLU   ma.

SOLEDAD   blu?

BLU   its gonna be okay.

SOLEDAD   it's just that . . .

BLU   i know what i'm doin. (*beat.*) you know, there some people never leave this neighborhood. live all their lives

inside a 10 mile radius. i wanna see, see the horizon. wanna
see where the horizon touches the earth, ma.

SOLEDAD   ay mijo. (*beat.*) you know, you'll always be
my baby.

(SOLEDAD *takes the milagro off her neck, gives it to* BLU. *He
puts it on.*)

SOLEDAD   had it blessed holy. on the back it says protegeme de mis enemigos.

BLU   protect me from my enemies.

SOLEDAD   i love you. (*beat.*) te quiero. i haven't
always . . .

BLU   sssssssssssssh. . . . i know ma. i know.

(SOLEDAD *and* BLU *begin dancing. Awkwardly at first,
like the first time she taught him how to dance at age 10.
She holds him, remembering. He holds her, trying to forget.*
BLU *spins* SOLEDAD *out his arms. Time/space change.*
HAILSTORM *picks up the dance.* HAILSTORM *and* SOLEDAD
are dancing alone.)

SOLEDAD   you got kids?

HAILSTORM   naw, girl. i ain't got no kids. don't know
nuthin 'bout raisin children.

SOLEDAD   sometimes, i don't think i know nuthin 'bout
it either.

HAILSTORM   sounds like you at a crossroads.

SOLEDAD   something like that.

HAILSTORM   we all make choices.

SOLEDAD   wutcha know about it?

HAILSTORM   nuthin. why don't you tell me?

SOLEDAD   long story.

HAILSTORM   i got all night.

SOLEDAD   hail?

HAILSTORM   yeah.

SOLEDAD   tell me about the moon. 'bout the aztec god of the moon. 'bout the time you went to mexico city. saw the temples downtown behind the church. 'bout how they built the entire city on an island.

(*trying to remember the story.*) lake . . .

HAILSTORM   texcoco. (*beat.*) when the spaniards came, they built their churches over our temples. but now the lake is draining, their churches sinking but our temples aren't. our temples are emerging from under the earth.

SOLEDAD   from underneath the concrete.

HAILSTORM   yes corazón, from underneath the concrete. when they were building the subway they found her. the god of the moon. buried underneath the earth.

SOLEDAD   the aztec god of the moon.

HAILSTORM   coyolxauhqui is the mexica god of the moon, eagle feathers in her hair, bells on her cheek . . .

SOLEDAD   the aztec god of the moon.

HAILSTORM   coyolxauhqui.

SOLEDAD   and the stars?

HAILSTORM   the 400 stars of the south.

SOLEDAD   they were guerilleras?

HAILSTORM   warriors.

SOLEDAD   and so was the moon?

HAILSTORM   the moon. she was the one, the one that fought against war.

(*Lights up on* GEMINI *alone on the roof.* LUNATICO *climbs through a second floor window, trying to sneak back into the house.*)

LUNATICO   where's ma?

GEMINI   out.

LUNATICO   hailstorm?

GEMINI   downstairs. waitin for ma.

LUNATICO   damn gemini. why you still up?

(GEMINI *ignores him.*)

LUNATICO   wutcha lookin at?

GEMINI   the stars.

(LUNATICO *stares into the distance, trying to see what she sees.*)

LUNATICO   i can't see shit.

(GEMINI *ignores him.*)

GEMINI   from up here, i can see the entire city.

LUNATICO   the entire city?

GEMINI   the entire city. north, south, east, west.

(LUNATICO *leans forward, finds himself in the sky.*)

LUNATICO   that's why you always up here, on the roof, gemini?

GEMINI   i like it up here. sometimes i come up here to remind me.

LUNATICO   'bout what?

GEMINI   that the world is so much bigger than our neighborhood, than our street. you know? sometimes, i'm up here on the roof and the wind blows hard enough, hard enough to knock me over. hair blowin, body leanin forward. sometimes, i have to hold, hold my whole body tight to keep from being pushed back. the sky turns neon when the sun sets. i can see it reflecting off all the build-ings downtown and the sky turns neon pink. from up here, you can't tell the difference between north and south, east and west. everything looks so amazing. you know?

LUNATICO   like, like when i'm at vato's grandma's house. she got a big ranch. no neighbors. at night you can see all the stars.

GEMINI   how many are there, luna?

LUNATICO   too many to count, gemini. you know, it
ain't like here. there, it's different. it's like the stars are
brighter there for some reason. at night, i'll lie down on
the sacate and just stare at the stars and sometimes i'll fall
asleep right there. and it's safe. i'm not even scared cuz
there ain't no neighbors and you feel like, you know, you
kinda feel like you high cuz you not really thinkin 'bout
nuthin, and it's like you high but you ain't. i use to think,
one day, i'm gonna live there on the rancho with the stars.

GEMINI   you know, sometimes, up here, up here, on the
roof, luna. sometimes, i can see, i can see blu.

LUNATICO   stop trippin.

GEMINI   blu's got wings. he's flying above us right now.

LUNATICO   he's gone.

GEMINI   nah, he turned into a star. some nights, some
nights, i see him in the moon, luna.

LUNATICO   stop it, gemini.

GEMINI   he's an eagle. wings spread, soaring. he lives, he
lives, on the edge of a cloud. when the sun and moon turn
bright, bright red, es él que pinta el sol, el sol rising and
setting.

LUNATICO   i'm fuckin goin to bed.

(LUNATICO *climbs through the window.* GEMINI *calls him
back.*)

GEMINI   luna?

LUNATICO   what?

(*Lights up on* SOLEDAD *as she enters the house.* HAILSTORM *has been waiting up.*)

GEMINI & HAILSTORM   where you been?

LUNATICO & SOLEDAD   out.

SOLEDAD   where's luna?

HAILSTORM   asleep.

SOLEDAD   where's gemini?

HAILSTORM   upstairs.

SOLEDAD   she should be in bed.

HAILSTORM   she waits up when she's worried.

SOLEDAD   what's she worried about?

HAILSTORM   you.

SOLEDAD   she out on the roof?

(SOLEDAD *calls out to* GEMINI.)

SOLEDAD   GEMINI?

GEMINI   WHAT?

SOLEDAD   WHAT ARE YOU DOING?

GEMINI   NOTHING.

SOLEDAD   WHERE'S LUNA?!

GEMINI & LUNATICO   IN BED!

(SOLEDAD *turns to leave.*)

HAILSTORM   where are you going?

SOLEDAD   to count my children. make sure everyone's home.

HAILSTORM   you ain't ever been a single mother, soledad.

SOLEDAD   what?

HAILSTORM   who cooks dinner when you're at work? who holds you at night? wakes up with you in the morning? who prays for you, soledad? hands open, kneeling at your altar. you have not raised this family all alone.

SOLEDAD   this ain't about that.

HAILSTORM   your children? i may not have birthed those children but i spent many nights when you was asleep and blu was out running the streets, trying to figure out how to make things right. but he never let me get close to him. he resented me for not being a man. i think sometimes luna does too.

SOLEDAD   it can't be easy for them to understand.

HAILSTORM   and what's your reason, soledad? cuz you ain't ever been in this alone. solita? no somos familia? what are we then?

(*Sound of a single gunshot. Helicopters overhead. Lights rise on* EME *and* SOLEDAD. *They yell over the sound of the helicopters.*)

SOLEDAD   not gonna teach my children to be scared in they own house.

EME   you need to put the kid's mattresses on the floor.

SOLEDAD   i ain't putting no gotdamn mattresses on the floor.

EME   being brave ain't no bulletproof vest. bullets don't got, don't got, names on them, soledad.

SOLEDAD   they ricochet off walls and can, and can, land anywhere, even if it ain't you they gunnin for.

EME   put their mattresses on the floor.

SOLEDAD   keep my babies safe.

EME   somethin's goin down, goin down, outside. you can feel it, feel it in the air.

SOLEDAD   it's hard to breathe.

EME   things change. there ain't no rules no more. more gangs, less turf.

SOLEDAD   used to be no drive-bys, no shooting into houses, no shooting at anyone if they's wit they family.

EME   used to be the challenge wuz one on one. those used to be the rules.

SOLEDAD   use to be i didn't say nuthin but i'm tired of the hard life. we got three kids now. i think it's time for you to quit, eme. time for you to quit the gang.

EME   our three kids are waitin for their dinner, soledad. wutcha gonna feed 'em? everything changes once money is involved.

SOLEDAD   no one ever gets forced in.

EME   you do what you do and you gotta live with the consequences.

SOLEDAD   or you do it different, you know.

EME   don't tell me what i need to do. i do what i do, just like you.

SOLEDAD   don't want my children learnin how to fold a bandana, the alphabet in gang signs, tatted up, wearin colors, and saggin jeans.

EME   you mean, you don't want your children to be me.

SOLEDAD   i mean, i want them to be able to dream, to have their own dreams, eme.

EME   can't feed your children on dreams, soledad. not enuf to keep 'em full.

(*Helicopters cut out. Lights up on* BLU *and* LUNATICO *on separate street corners. It is night. They are lit by the head-lights of an old Chevy. Shared memory with* EME. GEMINI *watches from the roof, unnoticed.*)

EME   roll the dice. roll the dice.

BLU   six. six.

LUNATICO   twelve.

EME   you get what you get. it's not like anybody got it in for you. it's a game of chance. count the numbers. add 'em up. one. six.

BLU   initiation.

LUNATICO   seven. seven times beat.

BLU   i rolled twelve. got beat up twelve times.

EME   sometimes you gotta learn the hard way.

BLU   don't get worse than that.

EME   insane. no brain. crazy ass barrio.

EME & BLU   204th street.

LUNATICO   pspspspshshshsh.

EME   hittin up,

BLU   strikin,

LUNATICO   crossin out,

BLU   roll calls,

EME   R.I.P.,

LUNATICO   rest in peace homie.

BLU   you gotta take it, right?

EME   be able to prove just how crazy you is.

LUNATICO   roll the dice.

EME   get what you get. it's not like anybody got it in for
you. it's a game of chance, right?

LUNATICO   five. five.

LUNATICO & BLU   ten.

EME   rocks, fists . . .

(*Spoken in the round.*)

EME	BLU
bleach, belts, boots	rocks, fists . . .

BLU	LUNATICO
bleach, belts, boots . . .	rocks, fists

LUNATICO   bleach, belts, boots.

EME & BLU & LUNATICO   rocks, fists, bleach, belts, boots.

BLU   metal tacks on knuckles

LUNATICO   held in place with scotch tape.

BLU   leather belts with silver studs.

LUNATICO   leather belts with silver studs.

EME   1.   2.   3.

EME & BLU   4.   5.   6.

LUNATICO, BLU, & EME   7.   8.   9.   10.

GEMINI   sssssshhhhhh.

EME   black ink tat on knuckles

BLU   carved in skin,

LUNATICO   tequila on the wound.

(*Call and response, voices build in intensity.*)

EME   suck teeth.

BLU & LUNATICO   suck teeth.

EME   lean back.

BLU & LUNATICO   lean back.

BLU & LUNATICO & EME   suck teeth. lean back.
throw 'em up. throw 'em up.

BLU   what? what?

EME   wutcha claimin? wutcha down for?

BLU & LUNATICO   i—am—a gangsta.

EME   wutcha claimin? wutcha down for?

BLU & LUNATICO   i—am—a gang—sta.

EME   wutcha claimin? wutcha down for?

BLU & LUNATICO   i—am—a gang—sta.

(*Sound of a single gunshot.* EME, BLU, *and* LUNATICO *duck,
out of sight. Lights up on* GEMINI *alone on the roof.*)

GEMINI   chain linked fence, clothesline, backseat of a
truck, pulled out/turned lawn chair, a pair of tennis shoes
left hanging. dance against the sky, blow away in the night.
rocks, fists, bleach, belts, boots . . . ssssh . . . ssssh . . .
ssssssshhhhhh.

(*A helicopter passes. Lights up on* LUNATICO *&* BLU.
Different time. Same story.)

LUNATICO   you know that cop?

BLU   which one?

LUNATICO   the one at my school.

BLU   walks around the school like he's the shit.

LUNATICO   short fuck.

BLU   carries a gun. hits the lockers with the night stick

LUNATICO   and he's always behind me, tellin me shit, like,

BLU & COP   get to class,

LUNATICO & COP   hope you not as messed up as your brother,

BLU & COP   i know your family.

BLU   he don't know shit.

LUNATICO   got caught taggin in the second wing bathroom and that cop, that cop got me written up as a gang member

BLU   for no reason.

LUNATICO   cuz i got a tag name.

BLU   we all got tag names. even the ones ain't in a gang.

LUNATICO   cuca, sin-a, casper, 1800s.

BLU   we've had tag names since we was in the 6th grade, right?

LUNATICO   right. and momma's been callin me gordo since i wuz a baby. so that don't mean shit.

BLU   but now your name is on some paper somewhere
next to the word

LUNATICO & COP   (*with contempt*) gang member.

LUNATICO   i'm in class when the cop and vice principal
come to get me, right. i'm sittin there thinkin oh shit, what
i do, right?

BLU   right.

LUNATICO   they call me to the front of the room and
ask me to empty my pockets.

COP   empty your pockets.

LUNATICO   so i do and i got

LUNATICO & COP   a blue marker

LUNATICO   in my pocket, right?

BLU   right.

LUNATICO   the cop looks at me and says,

LUNATICO & COP   this is contraband

LUNATICO   cuz we can't have markers at school.

BLU   now why can't we have markers at school? does that
make sense to you? there's a classroom in the second wing
with a broken window, bein held together with masking
tape. there ain't enuf money for books

LUNATICO   but we got enuf money to pay some punk
ass cop to worry about me and my gotdamn blue marker?

(*Lights up on* EME *and* SOLEDAD *in the past.* EME *tells the story to* SOLEDAD. LUNATICO *continues speaking to* BLU.)

EME   then he tells me to

EME & LUNATICO   turn around.

SOLEDAD   right.

LUNATICO   and he cuffs me.

EME   puts a pair of handcuffs on me.

BLU & SOLEDAD   in front of everyone?

EME   in front of everyone.

BLU & SOLEDAD   just like that?

LUNATICO   (*unbelievingly*) just like that.

EME   (*knowingly*) just like that.

LUNATICO   and i think they doin all this for a marker? but

LUNATICO & EME   i don't say shit, you know,

BLU & EME   keep your mouth shut.

LUNATICO & EME   keep my mouth shut, right?

SOLEDAD   right.

LUNATICO   then they take me into the office

EME   and that's when the cop tells me he's arresting me and i'm thinkin what?

LUNATICO   but i still don't say nuthin.

EME   just keep your mouth shut.

LUNATICO   you see, i know better.

EME   the cop, he takes me and puts me in the backseat
of his car.

LUNATICO   you know, i ain't ever been arrested before
and i ain't gonna lie, i'm scared shitless.

LUNATICO & <u>COP</u>   (COP *lines are underlined.*) the <u>cuffs</u>
round my wrists, <u>pinchin</u> my skin and my legs are <u>right up
against the backseat</u> and it's like i <u>can't move</u> and
i still can't believe this is happenin.

BLU & LUNATICO & <u>COP</u>   put a pair of handcuffs on
me <u>in front of everyone</u>. i <u>can't move</u>. i <u>can't talk</u>. i'm just
sittin there. the <u>cuffs</u> get tighter round my wrists. i know
not to <u>say nuthin</u> and the more i <u>keep quiet</u> the more an-
gry the cop gets. i <u>can't</u> say shit but i'm thinkin fuck you,
<u>fuck you</u>, fuck you motherfucker and i want to kick the
back of his seat but i <u>can't</u> even move.

SOLEDAD   i still can't believe this is happening.

(*Sound of the prison cell door closing. Lights up on* EME *inside
his jail cell.*)

EME   doors lock. slam shut behind you. 8 by 4 cell. you
a number now. it's how you will be identified. count off.
2878. gotta be careful. when you get out, cops will drop
you off in rival gang territory. make sure they all know you
there. one strike. drug conviction. your whole family gets
evicted from the projects. three strikes. you're out. it's like
they just waitin. just waitin for you to fuck up.

(*Lights up on* GEMINI *and* LUNATICO *on the roof. They are lit by a million stars.*)

GEMINI   luna, what you dream?

LUNATICO   don't dream 'bout nuthin.

GEMINI   you don't ever dream 'bout dad getting out?

LUNATICO   naw gemini. he gonna be there for a while.

GEMINI   don't ever think about him?

LUNATICO   sometimes i guess but not like a dream. you?

GEMINI   too young to really remember him much. sides i kinda like hail.

LUNATICO   she ain'tcha father.

GEMINI   didn't say she was.

LUNATICO   fuckin a woman don't make you a man.

GEMINI   why you gotta be like that?

LUNATICO   like what?

GEMINI   why you always gotta act hard?

LUNATICO   just sayin. (*beat.*) you always up here countin stars. it's like you's the only one that can see 'em through the smog.

GEMINI   what about blu? you ever think about blu?

LUNATICO   don't start that shit again, gemini.

GEMINI not asking you if you see him. askin if you think about him.

LUNATICO of course i do. all the time.

GEMINI (*beat.*) what you dream, luna?

LUNATICO told ya. i don't dream.

GEMINI being brave ain't no bulletproof vest. please don't tell me you don't dream. sometimes the dreams, the dreams is all we got, bro.

(LUNATICO *stares into the distance.*)

LUNATICO sometimes . . .

(*He stops.* GEMINI *encourages him to continue.*)

GEMINI sometimes . . .

LUNATICO sometimes i dream of leavin. city streets. concrete. bangin. all of it. stop fightin. stop frontin. just be.

(*Lights up on* BLU *in the past.*)

BLU stop fightin. stop frontin. just be.

LUNATICO & BLU sometimes. i dream of flyin. i don't even know where to. just flyin. my body outside this body. circling. i want to see where the horizon meets the earth. i want to dance against the sky, gemini.

BLU when i dance it's like i'm movin on water, ocean water so clear i can see the bottom of the sea and i'm so light i can dance on top of it all. on top of the water, against the sky. that's why they call it the c-walk. it's like you walkin across the sea. your full foot never touches the floor. stay up on toes or back on heels and pray, ocean waters carry me. i seen pictures, gemini, of oceans that are actually blue. waters so clear you can stand waist deep, look down and see your feet. not like any ocean i've ever been to. light reflects off the top of the water and you can see the sand on the ocean floor.

BLU & LUNATICO sometimes, i dream of flyin. i don't know where i'm goin really

BLU but the ocean water, she'll carry me. ocean waters, carry me, carry me home.

(*Sound of the helicopters in the distance.*)

LUNATICO gemini?

GEMINI yeah, luna?

LUNATICO you know. ain't no one ever ask me what i dream.

(*Light like moonlight shines on* SOLEDAD *and* HAILSTORM. SOLEDAD *is sitting between* HAILSTORM*'s legs. They are alone.*)

HAILSTORM close your eyes.

(*She kisses* SOLEDAD*'s eyelids.*)

HAILSTORM how many stars you see?

SOLEDAD too many to count. (*beat.*) you know, i wasn't sure i wanted to be a mother. after blu was born, i didn't know what else to be.

HAILSTORM and now?

SOLEDAD   there are some times that i just want to blow away in the night. want to dance against the sky, underneath a full moon.

(HAILSTORM *embraces her.*)

SOLEDAD   hailstorm?

HAILSTORM   yes corazón.

SOLEDAD   tell me about the moon.

(*The sound of the helicopters overhead. Lights fade on* HAILSTORM *and* SOLEDAD. *Lights up on* EME *in the past. He has been drinking all day.*)

EME   hear that?

(*Lights up on* SOLEDAD *in the past. She is tired.*)

SOLEDAD   what?

EME   the helicopters.

SOLEDAD   (*annoyed*) what?

EME   sounds like them helicopters gonna fall out the sky.

SOLEDAD   you're drunk.

(EME *begins raising his voice.*)

EME   metal birds in the barrio. huntin people like vultures.

SOLEDAD   stop it.

EME   they gonna fall out the sky one day.

SOLEDAD   don't raise your voice.

EME   someone's gonna throw a rock into the air.

SOLEDAD   the kids are sleeping. keep your voice down.

EME   the moon. the moon is going to break into a million pieces. fall into the ocean. the sky's gonna be black.
before there were colors, the sky was black, not blue. the
sky has always been black.

SOLEDAD   that's enuf, eme. that's enuf.

(EME *grabs* SOLEDAD.)

SOLEDAD   let go of me.

EME   no. listen. listen, soledad. the helicopters. the helicopters, sounds like them helicopters gonna fall out the
sky. you hear them? metal birds in the barrio. huntin
people like vultures. they gonna fall out the sky one day.

SOLEDAD   shut up. shut up eme.

(EME *pulls her hair.*)

EME   don't ever fucking tell me to shut up.

(*Lights up on* HAILSTORM. SOLEDAD *is holding her milagro,
round her neck. In silence, she remembers . . .*)

SOLEDAD   there's that split second. you know. that split
second before someone, someone hits you. you know it.
know they gonna hit you before it happens. see it in their
eyes. their body. whole body tenses up. hold it tightly. all
the years of anger and rage. disappointment. being looked
down on. thought less of. every time they got beat up.
beat down. the broken dreams. not wanting to dream big

because you might end up with big disappointments. not
wanting to dream at all. hold it so tight. the bones caught
in throat.

my dad used to beat the shit out of my mom and we knew.
knew when he was gonna hit her cuz the whole world
stopped, stopped spinning. that moment. even before the
fist is clenched. raised in air. that moment before. less than
a second. the spinning stops. he'd bite down on his lip.
open his hand. and pas. coffee table thrown. tv broken. on
the floor. silently. eyes closed fist clenched. pas. pas. pas.
and we'd sit there watchin. just watchin him wail on her
just watchin. and we's the only ones screamin. my sister
would hold me. i'd be all curled up in a ball. arms locked
round her neck. so i wouldn't see. tried to keep me safe.

i remember the sound of fist on face. and i knew. i was just
a little girl but i knew. i was never gonna let a man hit me
. . . until he did. until he hit me. gemini was just a baby,
just a baby when it happened. kicked and screamed. wasn't
gonna let her grow up like that. so when he got arrested.
that was it. that was it. no more. i wuz done.

HAILSTORM   (*beat.*) he's still their father, soledad.

(*Lights up on* EME *behind plexiglas.* SOLEDAD, BLU, *and*
LUNATICO *stand on the other side.*)

EME   thought i knew something 'bout family. thought
when you were family, you were family forever. blu, how
old was you when they took me away?

BLU   twelve.

EME   watched from the window behind white lace. tears
runnin down his face. gemini and luna was just babies. you
never once brought them to visit me. never returned my
letters. never even sent me a picture. i died that day.

EME & BLU & SOLEDAD i shattered into a million pieces that day.

EME and you acted like nuthin happened, like your children never even had a father. i didn't leave you. i'd never leave you. they took me. put a pair of handcuffs on me in front of everyone. the cuffs round my wrists were pinchin my skin. every time i moved, the cuffs got tighter round my wrists. and my legs were right up against the backseat of the cop car. i couldn't move. i couldn't talk . . .

why you here soledad?

SOLEDAD just didn't think it was right that they ain't ever seen they father.

EME took you a while, no?

SOLEDAD they here now, eme. aiiight. they here now.

EME you ever tell 'em 'bout me? 'bout how things use to be?

BLU never says your name.

LUNATICO gave all your clothes away.

BLU threw all your things out.

LUNATICO tore up all your pictures.

EME there some things you can't erase. i'm their father, soledad. it's tattooed in skin. homemade tattoo gun. made the motor with a walkman, held together with rubber bands to keep the needle from jumping. three small dots. you can barely see them but they there. family. brotherhood. the streets. those streets are home. they a part

of who we is. they run in the veins of my children. their
stories are written on the sidewalk.

LUNATICO like a tagger leaves his placazo.

EME   BLU
blu was eleven   luna was eleven
when he got his.   when i gave him his.

EME   and gemini . . . where's gemini, soledad?

SOLEDAD   don't wanna have nuthin to do with you.
nothing to do with any of it.

EME   there some things you can't erase. no matter how
many ways you try. they carry their stories, my stories,
with them, tattooed on skin.

LUNATICO & BLU   you can't ever take that away.

EME   you never even cried.

SOLEDAD   i don't cry.

(*Lights shift.*)

SOLEDAD   at night, i pray. when the sun falls out the sky
and the moon rises.

EME   at night i pray

SOLEDAD   i'm still at work

EME   i'm in jail

EME & SOLEDAD   but i pray. please lord

SOLEDAD   diosito santo

EME   dear god

EME & SOLEDAD   take care of my kids. can't stop, close my eyes, fall to my knees, look at the sky. no. i pray

EME   lying down in my jail cell

SOLEDAD   standing, in the factory

SOLEDAD & EME   eyes open. silently. no one hears but every night i pray.

SOLEDAD   please lord, diosito santo

EME   dear god

EME & SOLEDAD   take care of my kids.

SOLEDAD   when i get off work, i check their beds.

EME   three children. i have three children.

SOLEDAD   dear god, make sure everyone's home.

EME   soledad . . .

SOLEDAD   i gotta go.

(SOLEDAD *exits.* LUNATICO *follows her.* BLU *stays.*)

EME   blu . . .

SOLEDAD   blu?

BLU   give me a moment, ma.

(BLU *turns to* EME.)

BLU   you know sometimes, sometimes at night, sometimes i feel like no one cares about me. at night, when i'm
all alone, i turn on the radio, turn out my lights and just
listen to the words. you know, try not to, try not to think
about nuthin, 'bout all the shit. close my door, turn out
the lights, turn on the radio and listen to the words. eyes
closed and it's like nuthin can touch you, you know. you
don't have to think 'bout nuthin. and it's like you here and
not here at the same time and you can, you can just let go,
you know. no worries. just float. i spent my whole life,
spent my whole life, trying to prove there was a reason to
my being born. you know, sometimes i'm not sure that's
true and i try to, you know, hold it together.

EME   blu . . .

BLU   gotta go. i gotta go.

(BLU *turns the corner, deep in thought. He is caught
unawares. On the street, a group of boys.*)

ESE   wutcha lookin at?

HOMIE   where you from?

ESE   gang's name,

HOMIE   clique's name.

ESE   suck teeth.

BLU   suck teeth.

ESE   lean back.

BLU   lean back.

HOMIE, ESE, & BLU   suck teeth. lean back. throw 'em
up. throw 'em up.

HOMIE   wutcha claimin? wutcha down for?

BLU   crazy ass barrio.

HOMIE   insane.

ESE   no brain.

HOMIE   R.I.P.

HOMIE & ESE   rest in peace, homie.

BLU   "you're nobody, till somebody kills you."

(BLU *steps up to the boys. No one can touch him. Lights shift.
Music up. He begins dancing the c-walk. Gets lost in the
dance. Lights up on the* RECRUITMENT OFFICER. *Hands
crossed over chest. He's been watching from a distance.*)

RECRUITMENT OFFICER   what's your name?

BLU   they call me blu.

RECRUITMENT OFFICER   like the ocean?

BLU   yeah man. like the ocean.

RECRUITMENT OFFICER   where you from?

BLU   here. somewhere else i'm spose to be?

RECRUITMENT OFFICER   how old are you, blu?

BLU   eighteen.

RECRUITMENT OFFICER you graduate high school?

BLU yeah.

RECRUITMENT OFFICER what do you want to do now?

BLU i ain't really thought about it much.

RECRUITMENT OFFICER you gotta be goin somewhere.

BLU why?

RECRUITMENT OFFICER stand still, the world moves round you. don't wanna be a nuthin, a nobody. be a part of something.

BLU i am somebody. i am a part of somethin. where i'm from. that's what i, what i, believe in. you grow up in the hood. you're a part of it, it's a part of you. here everyone knows who you is and who you against.

RECRUITMENT OFFICER that's why you fightin? claimin streets? claimin neighborhoods?

BLU you gotta belong somewhere, otherwise you ain't nowheres. nowhere ain't no place, ain't no place to be. i'm from here. my homies they from here too. not from over there but from right here.

RECRUITMENT OFFICER don't you ever dream of leavin? city streets. concrete. bangin. all of it. stop fightin. stop frontin. just be.

BLU sometimes.

RECRUITMENT OFFICER tell me what you dream, blu.

BLU what?

RECRUITMENT OFFICER you ever think of joinin the military?

BLU what for?

RECRUITMENT OFFICER can't live your entire life hanging out on this here street corner. you ever been in a helicopter, kid?

you ever, ever dream of flying?

(*The sound of helicopters fills the entire sky.* BLU *looks up to heaven. Lights fade.* LUNATICO *lights a match. It goes out. He strikes another match, Lights a joint. Inhales slowly. Watches the smoke rise.* BLU *joins him.* LUNATICO *passes him the joint.*)

BLU graduate and everythin. can get good rank.

LUNATICO war in iraq. don't really like it.

BLU lot of older homies there. omar. carlos.

LUNATICO carlos's brother.

BLU all there.

LUNATICO heard.

BLU people in distress.

LUNATICO help.

BLU   over there.

LUNATICO   wouldn't wanna kill someone don't know.

BLU   you know.

LUNATICO   growin.

BLU   go huntin.

LUNATICO   teach you.

BLU   not kill somethin less you eat it.

LUNATICO   what we doin?

BLU   cannibals.

LUNATICO   why we killin?

BLU   didn't wanna go to war.

LUNATICO   gotta do what you told?

BLU   already signed up and everything.

LUNATICO   you know.

BLU   older brother.

LUNATICO   look up to.

BLU   just hope.

LUNATICO   there ain't war.

BLU   or nuthin like that.

LUNATICO hope.

BLU gotta. go. if there is.

LUNATICO yeah.

BLU just have to.

LUNATICO do it.

BLU if there's a war.

(*Lights up on* GEMINI *and* SOLEDAD *on the roof. Sound of the helicopters in the distance.*)

GEMINI hear that?

SOLEDAD what?

GEMINI the helicopters. sounds like them helicopters are gonna fall out the sky.

SOLEDAD what?

GEMINI one day, the stars are gonna become guerilleras.

SOLEDAD warriors.

GEMINI the moon she gonna break into a million pieces. fall into the ocean turn sirena.

SOLEDAD sirena?

GEMINI sirenas never die, singing underneath a black sky. one day, someone's gonna throw a rock into the air.

SOLEDAD make the helicopters fall out the sky?

GEMINI   yeah ma, they gonna fall out the sky one
day . . .

(*Lights up on* BLU *&* HAILSTORM.)

BLU   where's my ma?

HAILSTORM   at work.

(BLU *turns to leave.*)

HAILSTORM   where you goin?

BLU   out.

HAILSTORM   but you just got home.

BLU   so.

HAILSTORM   where you been?

BLU   why you care?

HAILSTORM   you know. your ma she's tired.

BLU   tired of what?

HAILSTORM   worryin.

BLU   what she worried about?

HAILSTORM   you.

BLU   ain't gotta worry no more.

HAILSTORM   why?

BLU   i'm leavin.

HAILSTORM   where you goin?

BLU   joined the military.

HAILSTORM   have you talked to your ma 'bout this?

BLU   i'm grown.

HAILSTORM   what you thinkin?

BLU   healthcare. education. benefits. they don't sell that
shit at the corner store you know.

HAILSTORM   naw but they be slangin it on the streets.
everywhere you fuckin turn in the barrio—recruitment
office. diversions game room—recruitment office right
next door. south park mall—recruitment office right inside.
the movies—recruitment office, same shopping center. not
enuf money for books at cha school but there they be.
posted outside the cafeteria. recruitment officers. they
sellin it, homie. just didn't think you'd be buyin it.

BLU   it's more than that. i'm tired too, shit. what i'm
spose to do? this ain't my house. not here wich you.

HAILSTORM   ain't tryin to be your father, blu.

BLU   cuz you ain't. (*beat.*) anyway—don't wanna wind up
dead or in jail. you know. not goin down. not goin down
like that.

HAILSTORM   we all got choices.

BLU   and i done made mines.

HAILSTORM   you know. i grew up never really havin a
home, never really havin family. runnin the streets to stay

away from the fightin. thought if i just kept movin. just kept movin. (*beat.*) you have a home, blu.

BLU   the military is like a brotherhood. forever. always faithful.

HAILSTORM   is a gang. shave your head cholo bald. turn in your colors for a uniform. get a new tat. it's not like you doin different. is still a gang blu. and 'sides we at war.

BLU   war's all round you. been at war my whole life. i fight it here or i fight there. all the same.

HAILSTORM   not the same. this is some street shit. that. that's real.

BLU   wutcha know about it? held my first 9 at 12. cold steel on warm hands.

HAILSTORM   stop frontin. you ain't ever shot nobody. lookout, distractor, driver. you ain't the one, the one that holds the gun.

BLU   forgot (*sarcastically*) you know what it means to be a man.

HAILSTORM   you want family? you *got* a family. *this* is your family, mijo.

BLU   MIJO?

HAILSTORM   i mean . . .

BLU   i ain'tcha mijo.

(BLU *leaves.*)

HAILSTORM   fuck.

(*Lights up on* SOLEDAD *alone on the roof.* LUNATICO *is sneaking back into the house. He doesn't realize* SOLEDAD *is there.*)

LUNATICO   fuck.

SOLEDAD   where you been?

LUNATICO   out. (*beat.*) where's gemini?

(SOLEDAD *ignores the question.*)

SOLEDAD   it's like i'm watchin my life on rewind. brother, son, father. a cd that won't stop skipping. LUNA i'm tired of watching the same movie over and over, por favor.

LUNATICO   turn off the tv then, ma.

SOLEDAD   don't be a smart-ass. you know, there some people never leave this neighborhood. live all their lives inside a 10 mile radius. they start to act like they own it. claiming streets. claiming neighborhoods. like it mean something to our family. to our people. those streets aren't ours. we don't own them. ain't no one come from the streets. i hate it when people say that shit. i mean, there are real people, real people, luna, that actually live in the streets. that don't have nobody, that don't have a family.

LUNATICO   don't worry. i got family.

SOLEDAD   tus amigos no son tu familia, gordo. este no es tu gente. i've had to be your mother and your father.

LUNATICO so what? now i don't got a father? i got
family, ma. nuestra familia. sides what you care? not like
you ever home.

SOLEDAD cuz i'm at work, cuz i'm at work, luna,
trying to make enuf money to keep you fed. hailstorm
and me . . .

LUNATICO so, now you and hailstorm spose to be my
real family? how you gonna try to teach me something
'bout family? my father's in jail. my brother's gone. you act
like nuthin's changed. just keep livin your life like nuthin.
like nuthin ever fuckin happened.

SOLEDAD you are my child, my son. (*beat.*) i'm your
family. you hear me? i'm your family.

LUNATICO you ain't my muthafuckin family.

(SOLEDAD *slaps* LUNATICO. LUNATICO *raises his fist to his
mother. Stops before he hits her. The earth stops spinning in
space.* SOLEDAD *does not move. Stares* LUNATICO *down. He is
shaking, fist clenched. Lights up on* HAILSTORM & GEMINI.)

GEMINI hailstorm, tell me about the moon.

HAILSTORM when they were building the subway they
found her. coyolxauhqui. the mexica god of the moon.
buried underneath the earth.

GEMINI i don't wanna be no aztec princess.

HAILSTORM wutcha mean?

GEMINI airbrushed on the hood of some lowrider or
printed on the calendar they give you for free at the
carneceria.

HAILSTORM   coyolxauhqui was a warrior, a guerillera.
eagle feathers in her hair, bells on her cheek.

GEMINI   eagle feathers in her hair, bells on her cheek.

HAILSTORM   skull tied to her belt. her brother, the
god of war, was born of the earth. skirt of snakes, hearts,
hands, and skulls. huitzilopochtli. a man. fully grown but
not. hummingbird warrior. he holds the fire serpent in
his heart. obsidian sword. handed down to him from his
father. his father's father. he gathered all the stars made
them soldiers. killed her. the moon. she was decapitated.
cut limb by limb. broke into a million pieces. and then
the fighting began.

GEMINI   why did she have to die?

HAILSTORM   not dead. she turned into the moon.
lights the sky.

GEMINI   not goin down. not gonna go down like that.
not this time.

HAILSTORM   wutcha mean, gemini?

GEMINI   why do we always end up killing each other and
our own dreams?

(*The sun slowly lowers from the sky. The moon rises. The sound
of drums in the distance. Drums become louder, fill the air.*
GEMINI *is dreaming.* LA FAMILY *create a large circle. Begin
dancing, counterclockwise. There is something ancient, cere-
monial in the dance. Shifts to more contemporary movement
and gestures. At the height of the dance,* GEMINI *dives off the
roof. Arms extended in flight. Lights out before she hits concrete. You can hear her breathing in the dark. Lights slowly
rise on* HAILSTORM.)

HAILSTORM   truth is—nobody wanted to be the indian
or the african 'cept the few of us grow up, try to find what
it is we missin, what got lost along the way and we try
goin back, try to learn the prayers and the rituals but
somethin ain't right in the incantation, in the conjuration.
it's like we lookin for somethin too far gone already and
come to find out, the indians and the africans don't want
us any more than we wanted them growin up. we're the
ones they sold after all, for gunpowder and rifles, the children of people displaced, searching for the traces of what
must, use to be, in the tattoos and piercings, in the dances,
the writin on the walls, the mourning of death airbrushed
on t-shirts, the rites of passage. searching for a time before
war but we can't think back that far and instead we left
with broken memories and broken prayers.

(*Lights up on* GEMINI *on the roof.*)

GEMINI   bright star in a dark sky. i dreamt i was the
moon, eagle feathers in my hair, bells on my cheek, coyolxauhqui. they buried the moon under the earth. my
brother he is the hummingbird warrior huitzilopochtli.
god of war. blue sun in midday. i sit here alone on the roof
listening to the helicopters, gathering the stars in silent
prayers. sun and moon. the earth she orbits, orbits around
her son. he carries my head, my head in his hand.

we've been dead. dead too long.

(*Lights up on* EME *in jail, reading a letter from* BLU.)

BLU   at night. in the dark. city lights. ruins of palaces.
destroyed. at night in the dark. the tigris river. rising in
the tauras mountains falling into mosul. tikrit. samarra.
baghdad. at night in the dark. flashes of light. sounds
i hear in my sleep. bombs dropping. children yelling.
drive-bys. flags snapping in the desert wind.

EME & BLU   at night. in the dark. it's hard to breathe
sometimes.

BLU   throat always dry. swallow the sand. caught in
throat. bones in back of spine. tears turn to stone. gray.

EME & BLU   narrow alleyways. crumbling buildings.

BLU   hot.

EME   endless.

BLU & EME   light. swift. accurate.

BLU   800 rounds per minute. feel the vibrations in my
body. my whole body shakes.

BLU & EME   can't stop. close my eyes.

BLU   spend most of my time

BLU & EME   not being me.

BLU   listen to the radio.

BLU & EME   think about home.

(*Lights up on* GEMINI *reading a letter from* BLU.)

BLU & GEMINI & EME   chain linked fence, clothesline,
backseat of a truck, pulled out/turned lawn chair, a pair of
tennis shoes left hanging.

BLU   dear gemini, i rode in a helicopter for the first time
today. from up here everything looks so amazing.

GEMINI & BLU   i can see the entire city.

GEMINI   north, south, east, west. hair blowing, body
leaning forward,

GEMINI & BLU   the wind blows hard enough sometimes to knock you over.

GEMINI   sometimes, i have to hold, hold my whole body
tight to keep from being pushed back.

GEMINI & BLU   the sky turns neon when the sun sets.

GEMINI   i can see it reflecting off all the buildings downtown and the sky turns neon pink.

GEMINI & BLU   from up here, you can't tell the difference between north and south, east and west.

GEMINI   everything looks so amazing. i come up here
sometimes to forget. i come up here sometimes to remind
me.

GEMINI & BLU   the world is so much bigger than our
neighborhood, than our street.

BLU   before i left, mom gave me this milagro. silver
charm tied round my neck. told me she had it blessed holy.
on the back it says

(*Lights up on* SOLEDAD.)

SOLEDAD   protegeme de mis enemigos.

BLU   protect me from my enemies. (*beat.*) remember
how she liked listenin to the jams old skool style. slow
dancing to *if you lose me you lose a good thing.* taught me
how to dance on the wood floors of grandma's house.
close my eyes. listen to the music. reminds me of my ma.

(SOLEDAD *begins humming, dancing slowly.*)

BLU told me no matter how old i got, i'd always be her baby.

SOLEDAD you'll always be my baby.

(*Singing.*)

nunca me dejes sola y sin ti
que sin tu amor no puedo vivir
because i love you i love you i do . . .

BLU toma.

(BLU *takes his necklace off.*)

BLU i want you to have it. cuz i know. i know how hard it is.

i'm sorry. i never told you i'm so sorry.

GEMINI sssssssssssh. (*beat.*) rocks, fists, bleach, boots. a group of homies form a circle around me.

GROUP OF BOYS (*Heard not seen.*) sssssssssssh.

GEMINI what's your name? where you from? where you goin? wutcha lookin at? where you live? i said no.

GROUP OF BOYS sssssssssssh.

GEMINI closed my eyes. sky black. my body outside this body circling. watched them. a group of homies. move closer. arms reach round me. push me up against the fence. broken pieces of styrofoam. caught. chain linked fence. an old pair of tennis shoes left hanging. throw me to the

floor. hard. lie me down. kicked and screamed. they
pushed up against my insides.

GROUP OF BOYS ssssssssssh.

GEMINI stopped saying no. tears turn to stone. i prayed.
lying down on concrete. hard. please lord disitio santo.

GROUP OF BOYS ssssssssssh.

GEMINI no one hears. no one hears. i pray. eyes closed.
dance against the sky. blow away in the night. back on
concrete.

BLU ssssssssssh.

GEMINI never. never told no one. never told no one no
one but you. you stood there. stood there. starin at me.
didn't say nuthin back. nuthin but

BLU i gotta go.

GEMINI never looked me in the face again. (*beat.*) i was
just a little girl.

1 2 3 4 5 6 7 8 9 10

and then you left

(GEMINI *puts the necklace around her neck.*)

BLU protegeme de mis enemigos.

GEMINI protect me from my enemies. (*beat.*) we've
been dead. dead too long. (*beat.*) it's time for you to let it
go . . . blu i forgive you . . . let it go.

(*Sound of the helicopters overhead. They cut out abruptly. Lights up on three* SOLDIERS.)

SOLDIERS we regret to inform you

EME another soldier died.

SOLDIERS we regret to inform you

EME his helicopter fell out the sky.

LUNATICO the stars became guerilleras.

BLU the moon fell into the ocean,

LUNATICO turned sirena

EME and now the sky is black.

SOLDIERS we regret to inform you

BLU ain't no one cared until he died.

EME now, he gets to come back a hero.

SOLDIERS we regret to inform you

EME three shots fired.

LUNATICO a trumpet sounds.

BLU an american flag

LUNATICO neatly folded into a triangle

SOLDIERS we regret to inform you

EME his body arrives today.

LUNATICO   ocean waters will carry him.

BLU   carry him home.

(*The sound of helicopters fills the air. Lights up on*
HAILSTORM *and* SOLEDAD.)

HAILSTORM   luna is trying to figure out what it means
to be a man. trying to find his own reflection in the faces
of other little boys.

SOLEDAD   can't raise his fuckin fist to me, hailstorm.
not in my house.

HAILSTORM   not in *our* house.

SOLEDAD   not in our house.

HAILSTORM   what you wanna do?

SOLEDAD   don't know what to do.

HAILSTORM   can't bury your not knowing. can't stay
stuck. not move.

SOLEDAD   you know sometimes after work, after work
i drive, drive into the hills. turn off my headlights. stare at
the lights. city lights from the hill's terrace. just think how
big the world is you know. wonder how i got here. why
here? this neighborhood, this street. sometimes i walk in
the hills, underneath a full moon. can hear the wailing at
night behind mission walls still standing. see the white
horses appear and disappear between buildings. there's that
spot where the tracks are at. a crossroads at the bottom
of the hill. they call that spot ghost town. say that in ghost
town, the children will push you over the railroad tracks.
the handprints of children left in dust, the handprints of
dead children, ghost children. i go up there. try to listen

to the voices of the ancestors in the trains passing. (*beat.*)
i ain't ever been alone. not really. first baby at seventeen.
moved from my father's house to my man's house. to a
house with my children. to a house with my children and
my lover.

HAILSTORM   your wife.

SOLEDAD   to a house always full.

HAILSTORM   soledad, let me love you. let it go. (*beat.*)
let yourself love luna. let me love you both. you're my
home, soledad. (*beat.*) we're a family. it ain't perfect but it's
ours.

(*Lights up on* LUNATICO. LUNATICO *is packing a bag. He is
running away. Lights up on* GEMINI *on the roof. She is building an altar.* LUNATICO *joins her, his bag in his hand.*)

LUNATICO   where's ma?

GEMINI   downstairs.

LUNATICO   where's hailstorm?

GEMINI   downstairs with ma. (*beat.*) where you goin?

LUNATICO   don't know yet. thought maybe vato's
house for a while at least.

GEMINI   ma is tired, tired of holding the sky.

LUNATICO   wadda you mean?

GEMINI   i am tired, tired of waiting.

LUNATICO   wutcha waitin for?

GEMINI   for the concrete to break. for the temples to
rise. for the moon to fall.

LUNATICO   i don't, don't understand.

GEMINI   i hope one day you will. night and day. sun
and moon. rising. *falling. rising higher. still falling.* i knew,
knew when blu left he wouldn't come back.

LUNATICO   how did you know?

GEMINI   cuz hummingbirds are not meant to fly with
helicopters. they cannot fly as high as the moon. my
brother, he carries my head in his hand. has to let go of
the hair from the roots.

LUNATICO   gemini . . .

GEMINI   i'm rewriting the myth. clipped his wings.
because this time i do not die. this time he was the ulti-
mate sacrifice. i cut out and eat his heart. even if more a
moment, the war will end. the moon will swim. i've been
dead too long. we've been dead too long, luna. i'm gonna
resurrect. gonna resurrect me. not gonna die. not this
time. not gonna go down like that.

(GEMINI *takes the necklace* BLU *gave her and gives it to*
LUNATICO.)

GEMINI   here. this is ours. it's all we got. take it.

LUNATICO   blu's milagro.

(LUNATICO *starts to put it around his neck.*)

GEMINI   put it on the altar.

LUNATICO   —

GEMINI let it go . . .

(LUNATICO *eventually drops his bags, not sure if he is staying or leaving.*)

GEMINI sky, moon, blue

(HAILSTORM, EME *&* SOLEDAD *appear in separate pools of light before they begin speaking. They are staring at the horizon.*)

HAILSTORM ocean blue

LUNATICO pair of pants, marker blue

EME bandana, sky, heart blue.

SOLEDAD blu.

HAILSTORM ssssh.

SOLEDAD blu.

HAILSTORM ssssh.

SOLEDAD blu.

HAILSTORM ssssh . . . ssssh . . . ssssh . . . ssssh.

EME
sound turns to waves
breaking

GEMINI
dance against the sky, blu.
blow away in the night, blu.

HAILSTORM ssssh.

EME
hitting the shore.

GEMINI
dance on the moon, blu.

HAILSTORM   ssssh.

EME	GEMINI
ocean waters so clear	close my eyes. see a million stars on the back of my eyelids, blu.

HAILSTORM   ssssh.

EME   you can see the bottom of the sea.

GEMINI   too many to count.

(GEMINI *lights a series of blue velas, until she ends up in a circle of candlelight.*)

LUNATICO   ocean waters carry you,

EME   ocean waters carry you,

HAILSTORM   ocean waters carry you,

SOLEDAD   carry us home.

(*Music rises. Lights fade.*)

c/s

Glossary

barrio	neighborhood
guerillera (s)	warrior(s)
sirena (s)	mermaid(s)
corazon	heart, dear
luna	moon
es él que pinta el sol	he is the one that paints the sun
sacate	grass
gordo	chubby
placazo	tag, mural
por favor	please
tus amigos no son tu familia	your friends are not your family
esta no es tu gente	they are not your people
nuestra familia	our family
solita	alone
mexica	aztec
diosito santo	dear god
milagro	charm/miracle
protegeme de mis enemigos	protect me from my enemies
velas	candle(s)

THE YALE DRAMA SERIES

David Charles Horn Foundation

The Yale Drama Series is funded by the generous support of the David Charles Horn Foundation, established in 2003 by Francine Horn to honor the memory of her husband, David. In keeping with David Horn's lifetime commitment to the written word, the David Charles Horn Foundation commemorates his aspirations and achievements by supporting new initiatives in the literary and dramatic arts.